Good Housekeeping
Cookery Club

CHOCOLATE

Joanna Farrow

EBURY PRESS
LONDON

First published 1994

1 3 5 7 9 10 8 6 4 2

First published in the United Kingdom in 1994 by Ebury Press
Random House, 20 Vauxhall Bridge Road, London SW1V 2SA

Random House Australia (Pty) Limited
20 Alfred Street, Milsons Point, Sydney,
New South Wales 2061, Australia

Random House New Zealand Limited
18 Poland Road, Glenfield,
Auckland 10, New Zealand

Random House South Africa (Pty) Limited
PO Box 337, Bergvlei, South Africa

Random House UK Limited Reg. No. 954009

A CIP catalogue record for this book is available from the British Library.

Managing Editor: JANET ILLSLEY
Design: SARA KIDD
Special Photography: GUS FILGATE
Food Stylist: JOANNA FARROW
Photographic Stylist: ROISIN NIELD
Techniques Photography: KARL ADAMSON
Recipe Testing: EMMA-LEE GOW

ISBN 0 09 178 995 8

Typeset in Gill Sans by Textype Typesetters, Cambridge
Colour Separations by Magnacraft, London
Printed and bound in Italy by New Interlitho Italia S.p.a., Milan

CONTENTS

COOKERY NOTES

- Both metric and imperial measures are given for the recipes. Follow either metric or imperial throughout as they are not interchangeable.
- All spoon measures are level unless otherwise stated. Sets of measuring spoons are available in both metric and imperial sizes for accurate measurement of small quantities.

- Ovens should be preheated to the specified temperature. Grills should also be preheated. The cooking times given in the recipes assume that this has been done.
- If a stage is specified under freezing instructions, the dish should be frozen at the end of that stage.
- Size 2 eggs should be used except where otherwise specified. Free-range eggs are recommended.

INTRODUCTION

For many of us, chocolate is the ultimate culinary temptation, unique in its inimitable flavour and texture. These qualities, combined with its irresistibly sweet, calorie-laden richness, have earned it the reputation of being 'wickedly good for you'.

CHOCOLATE PRODUCTION

Chocolate is produced from the beans of the cocoa tree. Originally native to South America, cocoa trees are now cultivated in several humid, tropical climates, including Africa and the Far East.

After harvesting the cocoa pods are split open to extract the pulp and beans. These are fermented in the sun to evaporate the pulp and allow the beans to develop their chocolate flavour. The beans are then sun-dried, ready for exporting.

The cocoa beans undergo several stages of processing to transform them into a thick, chocolate mixture known as 'cocoa solids'. This is then pressed, blended and refined to form the basis of the chocolate we buy.

TYPES OF CHOCOLATE

Generally the higher the cocoa solids content of chocolate, the more intense the flavour. This is an important consideration when buying chocolate for cooking, particularly when it is to be mixed with other ingredients which will dilute the flavour. Most chocolate bars specify cocoa solids content.

Bitter chocolate contains on average about 75 per cent cocoa solids. As its name suggests, no sugar is added so the flavour is remarkable rich. Available in some larger supermarkets, it's used mainly in confectionery and desserts.

Couverture chocolate also contains a high proportion of cocoa solids, and only naturally occurring fat. This gives a highly professional, glossy finish to melted chocolate decorations but it must be 'tempered' before use (see page 7) to make it easier to work with. Couverture chocolate is available in plain, milk and white forms, from specialist suppliers (see page 80).

Plain chocolate contains anywhere between 30 and 60 per cent cocoa solids, depending on the quality. Those brands with a higher proportion of cocoa solids give a richer chocolate flavour in cooking.

White chocolate derives its flavour from cocoa butter (extracted during processing) but has no cocoa solids. It is high in fat and sugar and should be melted carefully to lessen the risk of 'seizing up'.) It is particularly prone to this if melted in the microwave.) Luxury white chocolate brands are well worth using in cookery as they have a superior, less sickly, taste.

Chocolate flavour cake covering is available in plain, milk and white flavours. It is made from sugar, vegetable oil, cocoa and flavourings and is not generally recommended for use in these recipes as it has a synthetic flavour. A few pieces can, however, be added to chocolate when melted as the high fat content of chocolate flavour cake covering makes it easier to shape decorations, such as caraque and curls.

Cocoa powder is made by extracting some of the butter during processing to leave a block of cocoa which is ground to a powder. It is easier to work with than chocolate and is used in cakes and biscuits. Cocoa powder imparts a strong, bitter flavour but lacks the buttery richness of chocolate.

STORING CHOCOLATE

Chocolate should be stored tightly wrapped in a cool, dry place, away from foods with a strong flavour or aroma. Under these conditions it should keep well for about a year, but keep an eye on 'best before' packet dates. Incorrectly stored chocolate might develop a dull, whitish 'bloom'. Although still edible, the chocolate isn't attractive.

Intricate chocolate decorations, such as piped shapes, caraque, curls, ribbons and leaves, can be made in advance and interleaved between sheets of greaseproof paper in an airtight container. In a cool place, plain chocolate decorations will keep for 4 weeks; milk and white chocolate decorations for 2 weeks.

The following step-by-step guide to techniques will enable you to get maximum satisfaction from working with chocolate.

CHOCOLATE TECHNIQUES

On the following pages are step-by step guides to chocolate skills that are used repeatedly in the recipes. From simple basic techniques, such as melting chocolate, to decorative ones, like chocolate curls, ribbons and leaves, all the essential skills are covered. For decorative chocolate work, cool working conditions are essential. If hands are warm, cool them in a bowl of very cold water before you start.

MELTING CHOCOLATE

1. Break the plain, milk or white chocolate into pieces and put into a heatproof bowl. Place over a pan of gently simmering water and leave until melted.

2. Gently stir the chocolate until completely smooth. Remove bowl from pan, making sure that water droplets on the bowl do not come into contact with the chocolate. (This is particularly important when pouring chocolate onto paper or a surface for decorative purposes.)

NOTE: Chocolate can also be melted successfully in the microwave. Break into pieces and place in a small heatproof bowl. The time will vary according to the initial temperature of the chocolate, the amount used, and the type of bowl. As a guide, microwave plain or milk chocolate on HIGH, allowing about 2 minutes for 125 g (4 oz) chocolate and 3 minutes for 175-225 g (6-8 oz). White chocolate is best melted on MEDIUM as it is more likely to overheat.

CHOCOLATE MODELLING PASTE

1. Melt 125 g (4 oz) plain, milk or white chocolate in a small heatproof bowl (as left). Remove from the heat and stir, checking that no lumps remain. Add 30 ml (2 tbsp) liquid glucose or golden syrup and beat until the mixture forms a smooth paste which comes away from the sides of the bowl.

2. Transfer the chocolate paste to a polythene bag and leave in a cool place for about 2 hours until firm but pliable. (Or chill in the refrigerator to save time.) Lightly knead the paste until smooth.

3. To roll the paste, very lightly dust the surface with icing sugar. Break off a little paste and roll as thinly as possible to the required shape.

TEMPERING CHOCOLATE

Tempering chocolate makes it easier to use and produces a good glossy finish. You will need a chocolate thermometer (available from specialist suppliers – see page 80).

1. Finely chop 400 g (14 oz) plain, milk or white chocolate and place in a heatproof bowl. Melt over a saucepan (as left). Lightly stir, then tip three quarters of the chocolate onto a marble slab or cool, clean dry, smooth work surface.

2. Using a flexible plastic scraper, spread the chocolate thinly on the surface. Continue spreading and scooping up the chocolate to ensure that it remains on the move all the time.

3. Repeat this spreading and scooping action for about 5 minutes.

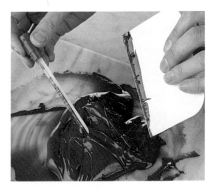

4. As soon as the chocolate registers 28°C (82°F), quickly scrape back into the bowl with the remaining melted chocolate and stir thoroughly. The temperature should be 32°C (90°F).

5. Put a little chocolate on the tip of a knife. If it sets very quickly – within a minute – it's ready. If not repeat the tempering.

CHOCOLATE SHAPES

1. Draw the required shape on a piece of greaseproof paper. Spoon on the melted chocolate.

2. Smooth with a palette knife to cover the required area. Gently shake and tilt the paper to level chocolate. Leave until firmly set.

3. Working quickly, invert the chocolate onto one hand and peel off the paper with the other. Use at once.

CHOCOLATE CURLS

1. Spread melted plain, milk or white chocolate in a thin layer on a marble slab or clean, smooth work surface. When only just set, push a clean wallpaper scraper across the surface of the chocolate at an angle of about 25°. If the chocolate breaks into brittle pieces, then it has become too cold and should be left to soften before trying again.

SIMPLE CHOCOLATE CURLS

1. Use a large chunky bar of plain, milk or white chocolate at room temperature. Shave off curls, using a swivel potato peeler.

CHOCOLATE CARAQUE

1. Spread melted plain, milk or white chocolate to a depth of about 5 mm (¼ inch) on a marble slab or clean, smooth work surface.

2. When only just set, draw a fine-bladed knife across the chocolate at an angle of 45°.

3. For two-tone caraque, alternate lines of contrasting chocolate on the surface. Continue as above.

CHOCOLATE SHAVINGS

1. Melt together 300 g (10 oz) white chocolate and 50 g (2 oz) white chocolate flavour cake covering. Stir until blended, then turn into a thoroughly cleaned 250 g (9 oz) margarine tub or similar-sized plastic carton. Chill until firm.

2. Turn the chocolate out of the container. Using a small knife, pare off paper-thin shavings, working with the blade almost flat against the chocolate.

TO MAKE A PAPER PIPING BAG FOR PIPING DECORATIONS

1. Halve a 20 cm (8 inch) square of greaseproof paper diagonally and use one of the triangles. Holding it with the longest side away from you, fold the right-hand point over to meet the bottom point, forming a cone shape.

2. Fold the left-hand point over the cone, bringing all three points together.

3. Fold points several times to secure.

CHOCOLATE SCRIBBLES

1. Place a little melted plain or white chocolate in a paper piping bag and snip off the merest tip.

2. Holding the piping bag about 2.5 cm (1 inch) above the area to be covered, gently squeeze the bag and move your hand quickly over the area to give a scribbled effect.

NOTE: This looks particularly effective if a contrasting colour of scribbled chocolate is applied to a chocolate covered cake. It is also an ideal way to decorate sweets.

FEATHERING

Feathering chocolate sauce on a plate makes an attractive presentation for a chilled dessert or individual cake.

1. Melt 125 g (4 oz) plain chocolate with 45 ml (3 tbsp) double cream until smooth. Spoon onto flat plates. Drizzle a little double cream (or melted white chocolate in a paper piping bag) over the sauce.

2. Immediately swirl into the sauce, using the tip of a cocktail stick.

PIPED CHOCOLATE DECORATIONS

1. Place a little melted plain or white chocolate in a paper piping bag and snip off the merest tip. Line a marble slab or board with greaseproof paper.

2. Pipe small decorative shapes onto the paper, keeping them reasonably small so they can easily be lifted from the paper once set. (If the chocolate flows from the bag too quickly, leave for a minute or two to thicken slightly).

3. Once the decorations have completely set, peel away the paper.

NOTE: Use piped decorations to add the finishing touches to cakes and chilled or frozen desserts.

STRIPED CHOCOLATE RIBBONS

To make these impressive decorations, you will need a few sheets of clear acetate (available from stationers). You will find it easier if you pipe and bend only two strips at a time.

1. Melt 125 g (4 oz) plain or bitter chocolate and 75 g (3 oz) white chocolate; keep separate. Cut clear acetate each strips, each about 15 × 5 cm (6 × 2 inches). Put the melted chocolate into two piping bags and snip off the tip from each.

2. Pipe three thick lines of the dark chocolate down the acetate strips, leaving a 5 mm (¼ inch) gap between each. (Pipe each line to within 1 cm (½ inch) of the ends of the acetate).

3. Use the white chocolate to pipe lines in between, to fill the gaps.

4. Leave for 1-2 minutes until the chocolate is cooled sufficiently to hold its shape, then bend each strip and secure the ends with sticky tape. Leave in a cool place or chill until firm.

5. Carefully cut the tape and peel away the acetate.

CHOCOLATE LEAVES

Use thoroughly clean leaves in perfect condition. Rose, bay, mint, lemon balm and lemon geranium work well. To cover 25-30 leaves you will need about 125 g (4 oz) chocolate.

1. Melt the plain, milk or white chocolate in a bowl. Using a small paintbrush, thickly paint the underside of the leaves with the melted chocolate. Avoid letting the chocolate come over the edges of the leaves, or it will be difficult to peel them away.

2. Place on a sheet of greaseproof paper and leave until set. (Larger leaves can be curved over a greaseproof covered rolling pin).

3. Carefully peel each leaf away from the chocolate. If the chocolate layer looks very thin, you may like to apply a second coat.

4. For variegated chocolate leaves, brush the middle of each leaf with white chocolate, then surround with plain chocolate (or vice versa).

DIPPED FRUIT AND NUTS

Choose small, whole fruits that are ripe but not soft. Strawberries, cherries, grapes, kumquats and cape gooseberries are ideal. Brazil nuts and pecans work well too. Wash fruit if necessary and dry thoroughly.

1. Melt a little plain, milk or white chocolate in a small bowl. Half-dip the fruit and, or nuts in the chocolate, letting the excess drip back into the bowl.

2. Place the dipped fruits on a sheet of greaseproof paper to set.

NOTE: These look particularly attractive served in a chocolate bowl (see page 64).

CHOCOLATE TRUFFLE GÂTEAU

This triple chocolate extravaganza provides the perfect opportunity to experiment with several decorative techniques. Layers of whisked sponge are alternated with a sumptuous white chocolate cream that's deliciously flecked with chopped truffles. This is then hidden under an artistic veil of finely rolled chocolate modelling paste. Cocoa dusted truffles and chocolate ribbons set it off in splendour.

MAKES 16 SLICES

75 g (3 oz) unsalted butter
6 eggs
175 g (6 oz) caster sugar
150 g (5 oz) plain white flour
25 g (1 oz) cocoa powder
TRUFFLES
150 g (5 oz) milk chocolate
90 ml (3 fl oz) double cream
15 ml (1 tbsp) brandy
cocoa powder, for dusting
FILLING
200 g (7 oz) white chocolate
300 ml (½ pint) double
   cream
TO FINISH
chocolate modelling paste –
   double quantity (see
   page 6)
striped chocolate ribbons
   (see page 10)
cocoa powder, for dusting

PREPARATION TIME
1½ hours, plus ribbons and
cooling
COOKING TIME
35 minutes
FREEZING
Suitable: Before decorating

390 CALS PER SLICE

1. Preheat the oven to 180°C (350°F) Mark 4. Grease and line a 23 cm (9 inch) spring-release cake tin. Gently heat the butter and leave to cool.

2. Put the eggs and sugar in a large heat-proof bowl set over a pan of hot water. Whisk until pale and creamy, and thick enough to leave a trail on the surface when the whisk is lifted.

3. Remove from the heat and whisk until cool. Sift half the flour and cocoa over the bowl and fold in carefully, using a large metal spoon. Pour the butter over the mixture, then sift in the remaining flour and cocoa. Fold in gently. Turn into the prepared tin and bake for about 35 minutes until just firm. Cool on a wire rack.

4. For the truffles, break up the milk chocolate. Bring the cream just to the boil, then stir in the chocolate until melted. Add the brandy and chill until firm. Shape into small balls and roll about 8 truffles in cocoa powder.

5. For the filling, break up the white chocolate. Bring the cream just to the boil and stir in the chocolate until melted. Leave to cool, then whisk until the mixture holds its shape.

6. Split the cake horizontally into three. Chop the un-dusted truffles and mix with half the white chocolate cream. Use to sandwich the cakes together. Spread remaining cream over the top and sides.

7. Take a ball of modelling paste, the size of a walnut, and roll as thinly as possible into a round. Crumple up slightly and press gently around the cake. Repeat with remaining modelling paste, overlapping the pieces, to cover the cake.

8. Decorate the top of the cake with the chocolate ribbons and truffles. Finish with a light dusting of cocoa powder.

NOTE: If necessary, secure the chocolate ribbons with a little melted chocolate.

TECHNIQUE

Cover the cake with the thin rounds of modelling paste, lightly crumpling them.

CHOCOLATE GÂTEAU WITH BRANDIED PRUNES

Under the disguise of a smooth, cream coating lies a wickedly rich cake to tempt all chocolate lovers. Moist plump prunes, steeped in a brandy flavoured syrup, are layered between the dark chocolate sponge rounds.

MAKES 16 SLICES

75 g (3 oz) bitter chocolate

175 g (6 oz) unsalted butter, softened

300 g (10 oz) light muscovado sugar

3 eggs

300 g (10 oz) plain white flour

5 ml (1 tsp) bicarbonate of soda

10 ml (2 tsp) baking powder

150 ml (¼ pint) soured cream

FILLING

175 g (6 oz) no-need-to-soak dried prunes

5 ml (1 tsp) vanilla essence

2.5 ml (½ tsp) cornflour

90 ml (6 tbsp) brandy

TO DECORATE

450 ml (¾ pint) double cream

250 ml (8 fl oz) crème fraîche

cocoa powder, for dusting

PREPARATION TIME
35 minutes, plus cooling
COOKING TIME
25-30 minutes
FREEZING
Suitable: Stage 3

475 CALS PER SLICE

1. Preheat the oven to 190°C (375°F) Mark 5. Grease and base line three 20 cm (8 inch) sandwich tins. Break up the chocolate and heat very gently in a saucepan with 150 ml (¼ pint) water until melted. Cool slightly.

2. Cream the butter and sugar together in a bowl until pale and fluffy. Gradually beat in the eggs, a little at a time, adding a little of the flour to prevent curdling. Sift together the remaining flour, bicarbonate of soda and baking powder.

3. Stir the chocolate into the creamed mixture, then fold in the flour and soured cream. Divide between the prepared tins and level the surfaces. Bake for 25-30 minutes until firm to touch. Turn out and cool on a wire rack.

4. For the filling, roughly chop the prunes and place in a saucepan with 90 ml (3 fl oz) water, and the vanilla essence. Bring to the boil, reduce the heat and simmer gently for 5 minutes. Blend the cornflour with 15 ml (1 tbsp) water, add to the pan and cook, stirring, for 1 minute until thickened. Remove from the heat and add the brandy. Leave to cool.

5. For the decoration, whip the cream until just holding its shape. Fold in the crème fraîche.

6. Spread the prune filling on two of the sponges, then cover with a little of the cream. Assemble the three layers on a serving plate and cover with the remaining cream, swirling it attractively. Serve dusted with cocoa powder.

NOTE: The prune filling, once cooled, should be very moist, with juices still visible. Add a little extra liqueur or water if it has become dry.

TECHNIQUE

Using a palette knife, spread the cream over the top and sides of the cake until evenly covered. Swirl attractively with tip of knife.

PRALINE GÂTEAU

A moist, dark chocolate cake – heavily laced with amaretto liqueur – is split and sandwiched with praline flavoured cream, then generously smothered in a glossy coat of indulgent chocolate ganache. For a special occasion, decorate the gâteau lavishly as suggested in the variation and illustrated in the photograph.

MAKES 16 SLICES

250 g (9 oz) plain chocolate
90 ml (3 fl oz) amaretto di
   Saronno liqueur
175 g (6 oz) unsalted butter,
   softened
175 g (6 oz) light muscovado
   sugar
4 eggs
150 g (5 oz) self-raising
   white flour
75 g (3 oz) ground almonds

FILLING
100 g (3½ oz) whole
   blanched almonds
125 g (4 oz) caster sugar
250 ml (8 fl oz) double
   cream

GANACHE
175 g (6 oz) plain chocolate
175 ml (6 fl oz) double
   cream

PREPARATION TIME
1 hour, plus cooling
COOKING TIME
1¼-1½ hours
FREEZING
Suitable: Cake only

545 CALS PER SLICE

1. Preheat the oven to 160°C (325°F) Mark 3. Grease and line a 20 cm (8 inch) round cake tin. Break the chocolate into a heatproof bowl, add the liqueur and leave until melted; stir until smooth.

2. Cream the butter and sugar together in a bowl until pale and fluffy. Gradually beat in the eggs, adding a little of the flour to prevent curdling. Stir in the melted chocolate. Sift remaining flour into the bowl and sprinkle in the ground almonds. Lightly fold into the mixture.

3. Turn into the prepared tin and level the surface. Bake for 1¼-1½ hours until well risen and a skewer, inserted into the centre, comes out clean. Cool in the tin.

4. For the filling, toast the nuts until evenly golden. Put the sugar in a heavy-based pan with 50 ml (2 fl oz) water. Heat gently until dissolved, then stir in the nuts. Bring to the boil and boil until the syrup begins to brown. Pour onto a lightly oiled baking sheet, leave to cool and harden, then crush finely.

5. Lightly whip the cream and stir in all but 45 ml (3 tbsp) praline. Split the cake into 3 layers. Re-assemble, sandwiching the layers with the praline cream.

6. For the ganache, break the chocolate into pieces. Bring the cream to the boil in a heavy-based saucepan. Add the chocolate, remove from the heat and stir until smooth. Leave to cool for 5 minutes, then whisk the ganache until glossy and beginning to thicken. Pour onto the cake and spread over the top and sides, using a palette knife. Leave in a cool place to set; do not refrigerate.

7. Sprinkle the remaining praline on top of the cake to serve.

VARIATION

Make the gâteau as above and cover with the ganache. Lightly oil several Easter egg moulds or 2 rolling pins, preferably in different sizes, and cover with cling film. Using a piping bag, drizzle melted chocolate randomly on the moulds or rolling pins to form lattice pieces. Sprinkle with the remaining praline. Chill until firm, then carefully ease the decorations off the moulds. Arrange on the cake, propping them against each other.

TECHNIQUE

Using a palette knife, spread the ganache over the cake in an even layer.

LIGHT CHOCOLATE FUDGE CAKE

This stunning white chocolate cake is a great favourite with chocolate lovers! Light sponge rounds are sandwiched together with whipped cream, flavoured with tiny pieces of white chocolate and lemon juice for a pleasantly contrasting lemony tang. The entire cake is covered with an irresistible white chocolate fudge icing and scattered liberally with chocolate shavings.

MAKES 12 SLICES

50 g (2 oz) white chocolate
4 eggs
125 g (4 oz) caster sugar
finely grated rind of 1 lemon
125 g (4 oz) plain white flour
FILLING
50 g (2 oz) white chocolate
150 ml (¼ pint) double
   cream
25 ml (5 tsp) lemon juice
ICING
175 g (6 oz) white chocolate
125 g (4 oz) unsalted butter
60 ml (4 tbsp) milk
175 g (6 oz) icing sugar
TO FINISH
chocolate shavings (see
   page 8)
cocoa powder or icing
   sugar, for dusting

PREPARATION TIME
35 minutes, plus cooling and
chocolate shavings
COOKING TIME
30-35 minutes
FREEZING
Suitable: Open freeze, then wrap
loosely in foil.

385 CALS PER SLICE

1. Preheat the oven to 180°C (350°F) Mark 4. Grease and line a 19 cm (7½ inch) round cake tin (see note). Finely grate the chocolate.

2. Put the eggs, sugar and lemon rind in a large heatproof bowl over a pan of hot water and whisk until the mixture has doubled in volume and is thick enough to leave a trail on the surface when the whisk is lifted. Remove the bowl from the pan and whisk until cool.

3. Sift the flour over the mixture, then sprinkle with the grated chocolate. Fold in lightly, using a large metal spoon. Turn into the prepared tin and bake for 30-35 minutes until just firm to the touch. Turn out and cool on a wire rack.

4. For the filling, chop the chocolate into small pieces. Whip the cream until it just holds its shape. Stir in the chocolate and lemon juice.

5. Split the sponge horizontally into 2 layers and sandwich together with the filling. Place on a serving plate.

6. For the icing, break up the chocolate and put into a pan with the butter and milk. Heat gently until dissolved, then stir until smooth. Beat in the icing sugar.

7. Allow the icing to cool, then beat until it forms soft peaks. Spread over the top and sides of the cake. Scatter lavishly with chocolate shavings. Serve dusted with cocoa powder or icing sugar.

NOTE: If you do not have a 19 cm (7½ inch) cake tin, use a 20 cm (8 inch) one instead. The sponge will be slightly more shallow.

TECHNIQUE

Using an electric whisk, beat the cooled icing until it forms soft peaks.

CELEBRATION GÂTEAU

This moist, dark chocolate sponge – rich with brandied raisins, walnuts and spicy ginger – is covered with soft almond paste and sealed in a sheer, satiny icing. Variegated chocolate leaves add the spectacular finishing touch.

MAKES 40 SLICES

225 g (8 oz) raisins
75 ml (5 tbsp) brandy
150 g (5 oz) walnuts
65 g (2½ oz) preserved stem
   ginger in syrup, drained
550 ml (18 fl oz) milk
30 ml (2 tbsp) wine vinegar
300 g (10 oz) plain chocolate
225 g (8 oz) soft margarine
575 g (1¼ lb) caster sugar
5 eggs
800 g (1¾ lb) self-raising
   white flour
65 g (2½ oz) cocoa powder
15 ml (1 tbsp) bicarbonate
   of soda
25 ml (5 tsp) mixed spice
150 ml (¼ pint) ginger wine
ALMOND PASTE
175 g (6 oz) ground almonds
75 g (3 oz) unsalted butter
90 ml (6 tbsp) stem ginger
   syrup
ICING
350 g (12 oz) plain chocolate
60 ml (4 tbsp) liquid glucose
2 egg whites
about 900 g (2 lb) icing sugar
TO DECORATE
chocolate leaves (page 11)

PREPARATION TIME
1¼ hours, plus leaves
COOKING TIME
1¾ hours
FREEZING
Suitable: Cakes only

460 CALS PER SLICE

1. Preheat the oven to 160°C (325°F) Mark 3. Grease and line a 25 cm (10 inch) and a 15 cm (6 inch) cake tin. Soak the raisins in the brandy for 2-3 hours or overnight. Chop the walnuts and ginger. Mix together the milk and vinegar. Break up the chocolate and melt in a heatproof bowl set over a pan of simmering water.

2. Put the margarine, sugar and eggs in a very large bowl. Sift the flour, cocoa, bicarbonate of soda and spice into the bowl. Add half the milk mixture and beat until smooth. Add the melted chocolate and remaining milk and stir until smooth. Stir in the raisins, walnuts and ginger.

3. Divide between the prepared tins. Bake the small cake for 1-1¼ hours and the large cake for 1¾ hours or until a skewer, inserted into the centre, comes out clean. Leave to cool in the tins, then drizzle with the ginger wine.

4. For the almond paste, beat the ground almonds, softened butter and syrup together in a bowl until smooth. Using a palette knife, spread in a thin layer over both cakes. Place the large cake on a board or plate.

5. For the icing, melt the chocolate with the glucose in a large heatproof bowl as above; cool slightly. Beat the egg whites until foamy, then stir into the chocolate with a little icing sugar. Gradually beat in more icing sugar, using an electric whisk.

6. When the icing becomes too stiff to beat, turn it onto a work surface and knead in enough icing sugar to make a stiff paste.

7. Roll out a generous two thirds of the icing paste on a surface dusted with icing sugar. Lift over the large cake and smooth over the top and sides, using your hands dusted with icing sugar. Cover the smaller cake with the remaining icing and carefully position on top of the larger cake.

8. Decorate the cake with variegated chocolate leaves to serve.

NOTE: This cake can be iced several days in advance and finished with the chocolate leaves on the day it is served. Apply a little gold lustre powder for a festive touch (see page 80 for supplier).

TECHNIQUE

Roll out the icing until 10 cm (4 inches) larger than diameter of cake. Carefully lift over the cake and smooth with icing sugar dusted hands for a satiny finish.

ALMOND, CHOCOLATE AND SWEET POTATO LOAF

Like cakes made with the subtle addition of carrots and parsnips, this recipe uses a puréed vegetable to both moisten and flavour the cake. Cocoa and delicious chunks of smooth milk chocolate give a light chocolate flavour which is nicely balanced with mixed spices and toasted almonds.

MAKES 8-10 SLICES

225 g (8 oz) sweet potatoes
75 g (3 oz) flaked almonds
125 g (4 oz) milk chocolate
125 g (4 oz) soft margarine
125 g (4 oz) light muscovado
  sugar
5 ml (1 tsp) vanilla essence
2 eggs
160 g (5½ oz) self-raising
  white flour
15 g (½ oz) cocoa powder
5 ml (1 tsp) ground mixed
  spice
2.5 ml (½ tsp) bicarbonate
  of soda
30 ml (2 tbsp) milk
icing sugar, for dusting

PREPARATION TIME
20 minutes
COOKING TIME
1-1¼ hours
FREEZING
Suitable

435-350 CALS PER SLICE

1. Peel the sweet potatoes and cut into chunks. Add to a pan of cold water, bring to the boil and cook for 15 minutes or until softened. Drain well, then mash with a potato masher.

2. Preheat the oven to 160°C (325°F) Mark 3. Grease a 900 g (2 lb) loaf tin and line the base and long sides with a strip of greaseproof paper. Lightly toast the flaked almonds. Roughly chop the chocolate.

3. Put the margarine, sugar, vanilla essence and eggs in a bowl. Sift the flour, cocoa, mixed spice and bicarbonate of soda into the bowl. Add the milk and beat well until smooth and creamy.

4. Stir in the mashed sweet potato, chopped chocolate and 50 g (2 oz) of the toasted almonds. Turn the mixture into the prepared tin and level the surface. Sprinkle with the remaining almonds.

5. Bake for about 1-1¼ hours until well risen and just firm to touch. Leave in the tin for 10 minutes, then transfer to a wire rack to cool. Serve dusted with icing sugar.

NOTE: Cook this cake as soon as you have mixed it, as the bicarbonate of soda is activated on blending.

VARIATIONS

If sweet potatoes are unobtainable, use parsnips instead. If preferred, replace the milk chocolate with plain. Substitute the mixed spice with 2.5 ml (½ tsp) ground coriander and add the finely grated rind of 1 orange.

TECHNIQUE

Add the sweet potato, chocolate and almonds to the creamed mixture and stir until just blended.

CHOCOLATE FILIGREE CAKES

Dramatically layered and prettily scribbled with chocolate filigree, these delicate cakes are most attractive. Cocoa flavoured sponge layers alternate with a filling of white chocolate, mascarpone and Greek yogurt for a pleasantly mild, cheesecake flavour. Chill for several hours or overnight before serving, to make slicing easier.

MAKES 16

2 eggs
50 g (2 oz) caster sugar
25 g (1 oz) plain white flour
25 g (1 oz) cocoa powder
FILLING
5 ml (1 tsp) powdered
   gelatine
100 ml (3½ fl oz) milk
200 g (7 oz) white chocolate
1 egg
25 g (1 oz) caster sugar
5 ml (1 tsp) vanilla essence
250 g (9 oz) mascarpone
   cheese
200 g (7 oz) Greek-style
   yogurt
TO DECORATE
25 g (1 oz) plain chocolate

PREPARATION TIME
30 minutes, plus cooling
COOKING TIME
12-15 minutes
FREEZING
Suitable

210 CALS PER CAKE

1. Preheat the oven to 190°C (375°F) Mark 5. Grease and base-line an 18 cm (7 inch) square loose-bottomed cake tin.

2. Put the eggs and sugar in a large heatproof bowl over a pan of hot water and whisk until the mixture has doubled in volume and is thick enough to leave a trail on the surface when the whisk is lifted. Remove bowl from pan; whisk until cool.

3. Sift the flour and cocoa over the mixture, then fold in using a large metal spoon. Turn into the prepared tin and bake for 12-15 minutes until just firm to touch. Turn out and cool on a wire rack.

4. Line sides of tin with fresh greaseproof paper. Slice the sponge in half horizontally and place one layer in tin.

5. For the filling, sprinkle the gelatine over the milk in a small heatproof bowl and leave for 2-3 minutes. Break up the white chocolate and melt in a heatproof bowl set over a pan of simmering water.

6. Whisk together the egg, sugar and vanilla essence in a bowl until foamy. Place the bowl containing the softened gelatine over a pan of simmering water until the gelatine dissolves. Cool slightly, then pour over the white chocolate, stirring until smooth. Whisk into the egg

mixture. Add the mascarpone and beat until smooth. Fold in the yogurt.

7. Spoon half the mixture over the sponge in the tin, then cover with the second sponge layer. Top with the remaining cheesecake mixture. Tap the tin gently to level the surface.

8. Melt the plain chocolate, put into a greaseproof paper piping bag and pipe lines all over the surface of the cake. Chill until required. Carefully remove from tin and peel away paper. Use a hot sharp knife to cut cake into 16 squares.

NOTE: If the cheesecake mixture becomes firm before you've layered the cake, beat in a little boiling water. If too thin, leave to firm up a little before layering.

TECHNIQUE

Pour half the cheesecake mixture over the sponge in the tin.

DOUBLE CHOCOLATE MUFFINS

Homemade muffins have a deliciously light texture that crumbles into soft, airy pieces of sponge when eaten freshly baked. This dark, chocolatey version is richly flavoured with melted chocolate; additional chunks of dark and white chocolate are folded in before baking, too. These give melt-in-the-mouth bites of pure delight!

MAKES 14

300 g (10 oz) plain chocolate
125 g (4 oz) white chocolate
375 g (13 oz) self-raising
   flour
15 ml (1 tbsp) baking
   powder
65 g (2½ oz) cocoa powder
75 g (3 oz) light muscovado
   sugar
1 egg
1 egg yolk
10 ml (2 tsp) vanilla essence
90 ml (6 tbsp) vegetable oil
375 ml (13 fl oz) milk
icing sugar or cocoa
   powder, for dusting
   (optional)

PREPARATION TIME
15 minutes
COOKING TIME
25 minutes
FREEZING
Suitable

370 CALS PER MUFFIN

1. Preheat the oven to 220°C (425°F) Mark 7. Line 14 deep bun tins or muffin tins with paper muffin cases. Break up 175 g (6 oz) of the plain chocolate and melt in a heatproof bowl set over a saucepan of simmering water.

2. Roughly chop the remaining plain and white chocolate. Sift the flour, baking powder and cocoa powder into a bowl. Stir in the sugar.

3. In another bowl, beat together the egg, egg yolk, vanilla essence, oil and milk. Add to the dry ingredients with the chopped chocolate and stir the ingredients together quickly until the flour is only just incorporated; do not over-mix.

4. Spoon the mixture into the paper cases, piling it up in the centre. Bake for 25 minutes until the muffins are well risen and craggy in appearance. Transfer to a wire rack and dust lightly with icing sugar or cocoa powder, if desired. Serve warm or cold.

NOTE: Unlike small sponge cakes, the muffin mixture should virtually fill the cases before cooking to achieve the traditional shape.

VARIATIONS

Add 5 ml (1 tsp) ground cinnamon or mixed spice when sifting together the dry ingredients.

TECHNIQUE

Spoon the muffin mixture into the paper cases, piling it up slightly in the centres.

GRILLED PEACHES WITH CHOCOLATE AND MARZIPAN

Grilled fruits make a remarkably easy dessert. Here, fresh peaches are partially coated in a glossy chocolate sauce, sprinkled with marzipan and lightly toasted until invitingly seared. Grilling emphasises the flavour of the peaches and slightly caramelises the marzipan, providing a lovely contrast to the tang of the lime.

SERVES 4

4 ripe peaches
125 g (4 oz) plain chocolate
150 ml (¼ pint) double
   cream
1 lime
50 g (2 oz) marzipan
30 ml (2 tbsp) icing sugar
TO SERVE
pouring cream
mint sprigs, to decorate

PREPARATION TIME
10 minutes
COOKING TIME
5 minutes
FREEZING
Not suitable

445 CALS PER SERVING

1. Halve the peaches and remove the stones. Arrange the peaches, cut-side up, in a shallow flameproof dish.

2. Break the chocolate into pieces. Pour the cream into a saucepan. Bring just to the boil, then add the chocolate and stir until smooth.

3. Pare thin strips of rind from the lime using a citrus zester; set aside. Squeeze 10 ml (2 tsp) juice from the lime and add to the chocolate sauce. Sprinkle a further 10 ml (2 tsp) over the peaches.

4. Chop or tear the marzipan into small pieces and divide between the peach halves. Drizzle a little of the chocolate sauce over the peaches and pour the remainder into the dish.

5. Preheat the grill to medium. Sift the icing sugar over the peaches. Place under the grill for about 5 minutes until the peaches and marzipan are lightly coloured.

6. Transfer to warmed serving plates and scatter with the pared lime rind. Pour a little cream onto the sauce. Serve decorated with mint sprigs and accompanied by pouring cream.

NOTE: Watch the peaches closely during grilling as they colour quite quickly.

VARIATIONS

Use ripe nectarines or pears in place of the peaches. You may need to take a thin slice off the rounded sides of the pears so they sit flat.

TECHNIQUE

Spoon the chocolate sauce over the peaches so they are only partially covered. Spoon the remainder into the dish.

CHOCOLATE BRIOCHE WITH POACHED PEARS

The gentle combination of syrup-steeped brioche, tender poached pears and chocolate sauce is invitingly reminiscent of a homely nursery pudding. Small brioches are available from supermarket bakeries, either in packs or sold separately. Alternatively, you can use toasted slices of brioche cut from a whole loaf (see variation).

SERVES 6

50 g (2 oz) caster sugar
1 cinnamon stick, halved
12 cloves
4 large dessert pears
5 ml (1 tsp) vanilla essence
6 small brioche buns
CHOCOLATE SAUCE
125 g (4 oz) plain chocolate
25 g (1 oz) unsalted butter
30 ml (2 tbsp) golden syrup
**30 ml (2 tbsp) double cream
 or milk**

PREPARATION TIME
25 minutes
COOKING TIME
6-8 minutes
FREEZING
Not suitable

415 CALS PER SERVING

1. Preheat the oven to 200°C (400°F) Mark 6. Put the sugar, cinnamon and cloves in a heavy-based saucepan with 250 ml (8 fl oz) water. Heat gently until the sugar dissolves, then bring to the boil and boil rapidly for 3 minutes.

2. Peel, quarter and core the pears, then cut each quarter in two. Add to the syrup with the vanilla essence and simmer very gently for 4-5 minutes or until just tender. Drain, reserving the syrup.

3. Using a sharp knife, cut off the top of each brioche and scoop out the centre, to leave a case about 1 cm (½ inch) thick. Arrange the brioche in a shallow ovenproof dish and pour a little syrup over each one to moisten (see note).

4. For the sauce, break up the chocolate and place in a heavy-based saucepan with the butter, syrup, cream or milk and 45 ml (3 tbsp) water. Heat gently, stirring until completely smooth.

5. Spoon a tablespoonful of the chocolate sauce into each brioche. Divide the pear slices among the cases. Bake the brioches for 6-8 minutes until heated through. Gently reheat the remaining chocolate sauce and pour over the brioches to serve. Accompany with pouring cream, if desired.

NOTE: Moisten rather than saturate the brioche with the syrup, otherwise they'll turn soggy and might lose their shape. Any remaining syrup can be added to the chocolate sauce in place of the water.

VARIATION

Instead of individual brioches, use 6 slices of brioche cut from a whole loaf. Toast the brioche slices and arrange the poached pears on top. Spoon on the chocolate sauce to serve.

TECHNIQUE

Cut off the top of each brioche, then carefully scoop out the centre, leaving a case about 1 cm (½ inch) thick.

RUM, RAISIN AND WHITE CHOCOLATE TART

In this delicious tart, a layer of rum-soaked raisins is hidden beneath a spongy almond topping, which is heavily specked with chunky pieces of white chocolate. These melt to an irresistible fudge-like texture when the tart is served warm. Crème fraîche is an ideal accompaniment. If you have time, steep the raisins in the rum overnight to allow them plenty of time to plump up.

SERVES 8

175 g (6 oz) raisins
90 ml (6 tbsp) rum
PASTRY
175 g (6 oz) plain white flour
pinch of salt
75 g (3 oz) unsalted butter
75 g (3 oz) caster sugar
3 egg yolks
FILLING
25 g (1 oz) unblanched
    almonds
350 g (12 oz) white
    chocolate
50 g (2 oz) butter
125 g (4 oz) light muscovado
    sugar
2 eggs
125 g (4 oz) self-raising
    white flour
TO FINISH
icing sugar, for dusting

PREPARATION TIME
25 minutes, plus standing
COOKING TIME
1 hour
FREEZING
Suitable

725 CALS PER SERVING

1. Put the raisins in a bowl, pour on the rum and leave to soak overnight if possible, or until most of the rum has been absorbed.

2. To make the pastry, sift the flour and salt into a bowl. Add the butter, cut into small pieces, and rub in using the fingertips until the mixture resembles fine breadcrumbs. Stir in the sugar and egg yolks, mixing to a smooth dough; add 5 ml (1 tsp) cold water if necessary to bind the dough together. Knead lightly, wrap in cling film and chill for 30 minutes.

3. Preheat the oven to 190°C (375°F) Mark 5. Roll out the pastry on a lightly floured surface and use to line a 23 cm (9 inch) loose-bottomed flan tin. Line the pastry case with greaseproof paper and fill with baking beans. Bake blind for 15 minutes, then remove the paper and beans and bake for a further 5 minutes. Leave to cool. Lower the oven temperature to 180°C (350°F) Mark 4.

4. Spoon the raisins and any rum into the pastry case. For the filling, roughly chop the almonds. Chop 300 g (10 oz) of the white chocolate into small pieces.

5. Break up the remaining chocolate and put into a heatproof bowl set over a pan of simmering water. Add the butter and leave until melted.

6. Beat the sugar and eggs together in a bowl. Stir in the flour, melted chocolate and three quarters of the chopped chocolate. Turn into the flan case and sprinkle with the remaining chocolate and the almonds. Bake for about 40 minutes until just firm, covering the tart with foil about halfway through cooking to prevent it overbrowning. Serve warm, dusted with icing sugar.

VARIATIONS

Replace the raisins and rum with sultanas and amaretto liqueur. Use milk or plain rather than white chocolate.

TECHNIQUE

Spoon the raisins and any remaining rum in an even layer over the pastry case.

CHOCOLATE BLINIS WITH HAZELNUT CARAMEL

Old fashioned drop scones take on a new lease of life in this pudding. The combination of melting chocolate oozing from the blinis, tangy nut caramel and creamy yogurt is sheer bliss! Both the batter and sauce can be made in advance. You may also prefer to cook the blinis ahead and reheat them in the oven just before serving.

SERVES 6

75 g (3 oz) milk chocolate
100 g (3½ oz) self-raising
   white flour
15 g (½ oz) cocoa powder
2.5 ml (½ tsp) baking
   powder
15 ml (1 tbsp) caster sugar
1 egg
200 ml (7 fl oz) milk
a little oil, for cooking
SAUCE
50 g (2 oz) shelled hazelnuts
75 g (3 oz) caster sugar
grated rind of ½ orange
40 g (1½ oz) unsalted butter
TO SERVE
Greek-style yogurt

PREPARATION TIME
15 minutes
COOKING TIME
20 minutes
FREEZING
Not suitable

350 CALS PER SERVING

1. Roughly chop the chocolate. Sift the flour, cocoa powder and baking powder into a bowl. Stir in the sugar. Make a well in the centre and stir in the egg and a little of the milk to make a thick batter. Stir in the remaining milk and the chopped chocolate. Leave to stand while making the sauce.

2. Preheat the grill. Chop the nuts very roughly and toast, turning frequently, until evenly golden. Put the sugar in a small heavy-based pan with 90 ml (3 fl oz) water and heat gently until the sugar dissolves. Bring to the boil and boil rapidly until deep golden. Immerse the base of the pan in cold water to prevent further cooking.

3. Carefully add 30 ml (2 tbsp) water, standing back as the syrup will splutter. Add the hazelnuts, orange rind and butter, and reheat gently until smooth and glossy.

4. Cook the blinis in batches. Heat a little oil in a large frying pan or griddle over a moderate heat. Add dessert-spoonfuls of the batter, spacing them well apart. Fry gently for 2 minutes or until bubbles appear on the surface. Flip the blinis over with a palette knife and cook until just firm. Transfer to a warmed plate.

5. Gently reheat the sauce. Transfer the blinis to serving plates, allowing three each, and pour a little of the sauce over them. Serve immediately, with yogurt.

NOTE: The blinis can be cooked in advance and reheated in the oven just before serving. Interleave with grease-proof paper as you cook them. To serve, wrap in greaseproof paper and warm through in a preheated oven at 180°C (350°F) Mark 4 for 10 minutes.

VARIATIONS

Use toasted walnuts or almonds in place of the hazelnuts and lemon instead of the orange rind. Soured cream or crème fraîche can be served instead of yogurt.

TECHNIQUE

Cook the blinis until large bubbles appear on the surface, then flip over using a palette knife.

STICKY DATE AND ORANGE PUDDING

Wallow in glorious indulgence with this steaming hot, wintery dessert. Distinctly flavoured with oranges, dates and flecks of white chocolate, the light-textured spongy pudding is served topped with a delicious toffee sauce. Serve with custard or pouring cream.

SERVES 6

175 g (6 oz) stoned dates

150 ml (¼ pint) fresh orange juice

50 g (2 oz) white chocolate

75 g (3 oz) unsalted butter, softened

150 g (5 oz) light muscovado sugar

2 eggs

150 g (5 oz) self-raising white flour

25 g (1 oz) cocoa powder

2.5 ml (½ tsp) bicarbonate of soda

grated rind of 1 orange

SAUCE

125 g (4 oz) light muscovado sugar

75 g (3 oz) unsalted butter

60 ml (4 tbsp) double cream

15 ml (1 tbsp) lemon juice

TO SERVE

pouring cream or custard

PREPARATION TIME
20 minutes
COOKING TIME
2 hours
FREEZING
Not suitable

625 CALS PER SERVING

1. Butter a 1.4 litre (2½ pint) pudding basin and line the base with a circle of greaseproof paper. Roughly chop the dates and place in a saucepan with the orange juice. Bring to the boil, reduce the heat and simmer gently for 5 minutes. Leave to cool while preparing the pudding.

2. Roughly chop the white chocolate. Put the butter, sugar and eggs in a large bowl. Sift the flour, cocoa powder and bicarbonate of soda into the bowl and beat well until evenly combined.

3. Remove one third of the date pieces from the saucepan, using a slotted spoon; set aside. Add the remaining dates and orange juice to the pudding mixture with the orange rind and chopped chocolate. Stir well, then turn into the prepared basin.

4. Cover the basin with a double thickness of greaseproof paper and sheet of foil. Secure under the rim with string. Place in a steamer and add boiling water. Cover and steam for 2 hours. Top up with more boiling water as necessary during cooking.

5. Meanwhile, make the sauce. Put the sugar, butter and cream in a small pan. Heat gently until the sugar dissolves, then stir in the reserved dates and lemon juice. Boil for 1 minute.

6. Remove the pudding from steamer and invert onto a serving plate. Pour toffee sauce over the pudding to coat evenly. Hand any remaining sauce separately. Serve with pouring cream or custard.

NOTE: If you don't have a steamer, rest the pudding basin on an upturned old saucer in a large saucepan. Pour sufficient boiling water into the pan to come halfway up the sides of the basin.

VARIATIONS

Use chopped prunes, figs or pears in place of the dates.

TECHNIQUE

Cover the pudding basin with greased greaseproof paper, then a layer of foil. Secure under the rim with string.

CHOCOLATE BREAD AND BUTTER PUDDING

This irresistible recipe has all the comforting qualities of a traditional bread and butter pudding – it's sweet, eggy, soft-textured and so difficult to resist. The bonus here is the generous pockets of dark, gooey chocolate sauce, melting into the spiced vanilla custard to create a perfect balance of flavours.

SERVES 6

200 g (7 oz) plain chocolate
75 g (3 oz) unsalted butter
225 g (8 oz) fruited bun loaf
or light teabread
5 ml (1 tsp) vanilla essence
2.5 ml (½ tsp) ground
cinnamon
3 eggs
25 g (1 oz) caster sugar
600 ml (1 pint) milk
cocoa powder and icing
sugar, for dusting

PREPARATION TIME
15 minutes, plus standing
COOKING TIME
45-55 minutes
FREEZING
Not suitable

500 CALS PER SERVING

1. Lightly grease the sides of a 1.7 litre (3 pint) ovenproof dish. Break up the chocolate and put into a heatproof bowl set over a pan of simmering water. Add 25 g (1 oz) of the butter and leave until melted. Stir lightly.

2. Cut the fruited bread into thin slices and arrange a third of the slices, overlapping, in the prepared dish. Spread with half the chocolate sauce. Arrange half the remaining bread in the dish and spread with the remaining sauce. Finally arrange the last of the bread slices in the dish.

3. Melt the remaining butter. Remove from the heat and stir in the vanilla essence, cinnamon, eggs, sugar and milk. Beat thoroughly, then pour over the bread. Leave to stand for 1 hour until the bread has softened. Preheat the oven to 180°C (350°F) Mark 4.

4. Bake the pudding in the oven for 45-55 minutes until the custard has set and the bread is deep golden brown. Leave to stand for 5 minutes. Dust with cocoa powder and icing sugar before serving.

NOTE: Use a teabread that's lightly dotted with fruits, otherwise the pudding will be too heavy. Allow to stand for a full 1 hour before baking to ensure a really good texture.

VARIATION

Substitute the fruited bread with brioche or ordinary unsliced bread. Lightly scatter with raisins when layering the bread in the dish.

TECHNIQUE

Spoon half the chocolate sauce over the first layer of bread slices in the dish.

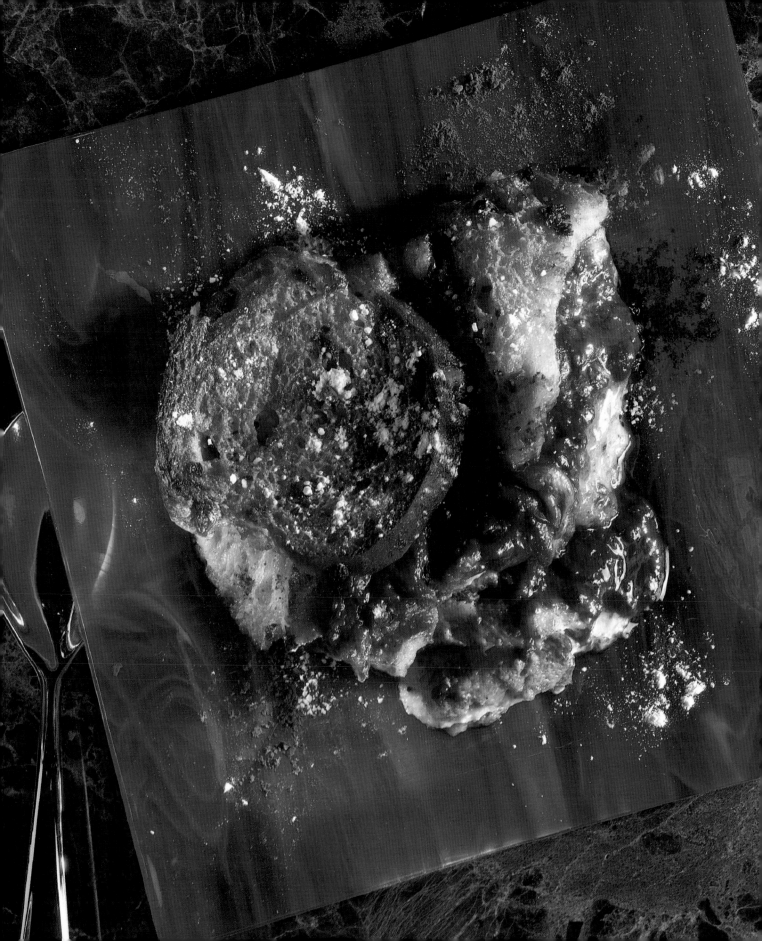

CHOCOLATE, WALNUT AND MAPLE PUDDINGS

Unlike most steamed puds, these pretty individual ones are made from a whisked mixture – of eggs, cocoa, walnuts and ground almonds – resulting in an exceptionally light, soufflé-like texture. Serve freshly steamed or, for convenience, make ahead and freeze unbaked.

SERVES 8

50 g (2 oz) shelled walnuts

150 g (5 oz) unsalted butter, softened

175 g (6 oz) light muscovado sugar

1.25 ml (¼ tsp) ground nutmeg

25 g (1 oz) plain white flour

60 ml (4 tbsp) cocoa powder

5 eggs, separated

125 g (4 oz) ground almonds

50 g (2 oz) breadcrumbs

TO SERVE

crème fraîche

maple syrup

extra chopped walnuts, for sprinkling

PREPARATION TIME
25 minutes
COOKING TIME
30 minutes
FREEZING
Suitable: Stage 4. Bake from frozen, allowing an extra 5 minutes.

525 CALS PER SERVING

1. Preheat the oven to 180°C (350°F) Mark 4. Grease 8 individual pudding basins and line the bases with grease-proof paper.

2. Chop the walnuts. In a bowl, cream the butter with 50 g (2 oz) of the sugar and the nutmeg until fluffy. Sift the flour and cocoa into the bowl. Add the egg yolks, ground almonds, breadcrumbs and nuts and stir until just combined.

3. Whisk the egg whites until stiff. Gradually whisk in the remaining sugar. Fold a quarter into the chocolate mixture, to lighten it, using a metal spoon. Carefully fold in the remaining mixture.

4. Spoon the mixture into the prepared basins, filling them no more than two-thirds full.

5. Stand the pudding basins in a roasting tin and pour in sufficient boiling water to give a 1 cm (½ inch) depth. Cover the tin completely with foil and bake for 30 minutes or until the puddings feel firm.

6. Loosen the edges of the puddings with a knife and turn out onto warmed serving plates. Put a spoonful of crème fraîche beside each pudding. Drizzle with maple syrup and sprinkle with chopped walnuts to serve.

TECHNIQUE

Using a large metal spoon, carefully fold the whisked egg whites into the chocolate mixture until just incorporated.

HOT CHERRY AND CHOCOLATE TRIFLE

The slightly sour taste of fresh cherries is traditionally partnered with chocolate in several classic dishes. Here, the combination is used to update an old favourite. Pitted cherries are mixed with liqueur-steeped amaretti biscuits and toasted almonds, then baked under a blanket of glossy chocolate, mascarpone and cream sauce.

SERVES 6

450 g (1 lb) fresh cherries, or two 425 g (15 oz) cans pitted cherries
50 g (2 oz) blanched almonds
60 ml (4 tbsp) sweet sherry or amaretto di Saronno liqueur
150 ml (¼ pint) freshly squeezed orange juice
grated rind of 1 orange
2.5 ml (½ tsp) almond essence
175 g (6 oz) amaretti biscuits
175 g (6 oz) plain chocolate
2.5 ml (½ tsp) cornflour
90 ml (3 fl oz) double cream
250 g (9 oz) mascarpone cheese
TO SERVE
icing sugar, for dusting
lightly whipped cream

PREPARATION TIME
30 minutes
COOKING TIME
25 minutes
FREEZING
Not suitable

635 CALS PER SERVING

1. Preheat the oven to 200°C (400°F) Mark 6. Wash and stone the fresh cherries, or thoroughly drain canned ones. Preheat the grill and lightly toast the almonds, then roughly chop them.

2. Scatter half the cherries in the base of a 1.7 litre (3 pint) ovenproof dish and drizzle with the sherry or liqueur.

3. In a shallow dish, mix together the orange juice, orange rind and almond essence. Dip the biscuits into the mixture until moistened but not saturated, then arrange over the cherries in the dish. Scatter the remaining cherries on top. Sprinkle with two thirds of the almonds and bake for 15 minutes.

4. Meanwhile, break up the chocolate. Blend the cornflour with a little of the cream in a small saucepan, then stir in the remaining cream. Add the chocolate and stir over a gentle heat, until the chocolate has melted.

5. Lightly whisk the mascarpone in a bowl to loosen it, then gradually whisk in the chocolate sauce. Pour over the trifle and sprinkle with the remaining almonds. Return to the oven for a further 10 minutes. Dust with icing sugar and serve hot, with cream.

VARIATION

Use 6 individual ovenproof glass dishes rather than one large one and reduce the initial cooking time by 5 minutes.

TECHNIQUE

Dip the amaretti biscuits in the orange juice mixture until moistened but not saturated, then arrange over the layer of cherries.

ROSEMARY POACHED PEARS WITH CHOCOLATE SAUCE

The wonderfully warm, heady scent and flavour of fresh rosemary has a great affinity with sweet dishes. Here, dessert pears are poached in syrup with almondy amaretto and rosemary, producing a perfectly balanced combination of flavours. A smooth, glossy chocolate sauce adds the perfect finishing touch.

SERVES 6

12 small pears (see note)
30 ml (2 tbsp) lemon juice
200 g (7 oz) caster sugar
4-5 fresh rosemary sprigs,
    each 7.5 cm (3 inches)
    long
45 ml (3 tbsp) amaretto di
    Saronno liqueur
SAUCE
200 g (7 oz) plain or bitter
    chocolate
150 ml (¼ pint) double
    cream
TO SERVE
toasted flaked almonds, for
    sprinkling
rosemary sprigs, to
    decorate

PREPARATION TIME
20 minutes, plus cooling
COOKING TIME
20-25 minutes
FREEZING
Not suitable

555 CALS PER SERVING

1. Peel the pears, leaving them whole with the stalks intact. Using the tip of a potato peeler, scoop out the core end from each pear. Brush the pears with the lemon juice to prevent discolouration.

2. Put the sugar in a large heavy-based saucepan with 450 ml (¾ pint) water and the rosemary sprigs. Heat gently until the sugar dissolves, then bring to the boil and boil for 1 minute until syrupy. Stir in the liqueur. Add the pears, packing them in as snugly as possible. Cover and simmer for 20-25 minutes, turning the pears in the syrup occasionally.

3. Transfer the pears to a glass bowl, using a slotted spoon. Boil the syrup for 2 minutes to reduce and thicken slightly. Discard the rosemary, then pour the syrup over the pears and allow to cool.

4. To make the sauce, break up the chocolate and put into a large heatproof bowl. Bring the cream to the boil in a saucepan, then pour over the chocolate. Leave until the chocolate has melted, then stir gently until smooth.

5. Arrange 2 pears on each serving plate and spoon on a little syrup. Sprinkle with the toasted almonds and decorate with rosemary sprigs. Serve at once, with the chocolate sauce.

NOTE: Use any very small, ripe dessert pears. Avoid over-ripe ones which will quickly turn mushy and cloud the syrup. If small pears are unobtainable, use medium ones and allow one per person.

TECHNIQUE

Use the tip of a potato peeler to twist out the core end of each pear.

CHOCOLATE LACE VASES WITH COCONUT CUSTARD

In this elegant dessert, creamy coconut milk is used as the base of a velvety smooth custard. This is spooned into prettily fluted lace biscuits, lightly flavoured with cocoa and brandy, and set off with a scattering of toasted coconut and chocolate curls. Both vases and custard can be made a day in advance; assemble just before serving.

SERVES 8

LACE VASES

75 g (3 oz) unsalted butter
75 g (3 oz) caster sugar
45 ml (3 tbsp) golden syrup
65 g (2½ oz) plain white flour
15 g (½ oz) cocoa powder
30 ml (2 tbsp) brandy
125 g (4 oz) milk chocolate

COCONUT CUSTARD

2 egg yolks
50 g (2 oz) caster sugar
25 g (1 oz) cornflour
60 ml (4 tbsp) milk
2.5 ml (¼ tsp) vanilla essence
150 ml (¼ pint) double cream
400 ml (14 fl oz) can coconut milk
15 ml (1 tbsp) lemon juice

TO DECORATE

cocoa powder, for dusting
chocolate curls (see page 8)
toasted coconut shavings (see note)

PREPARATION TIME
45 minutes, plus chocolate curls
COOKING TIME
About 25 minutes
FREEZING
Not suitable

550 CALS PER SERVING

1. For the lace vases, preheat the oven to 190°C (375°F) Mark 5. Grease a baking sheet and line with non-stick baking parchment. Melt the butter with the sugar and syrup in a small saucepan. Remove from the heat and stir in the flour, cocoa and brandy until smooth.

2. Cover a small, slender egg cup (or similar-sized container) with foil. Place 2 separate tablespoons of the mixture, spaced well apart, on the baking sheet. Bake for 5-8 minutes or until spread to a thin layer with a lacy texture. Remove from the oven and leave for 15-30 seconds.

3. Loosen the edges with a palette knife, then lift one of the biscuits over the foil-covered cup. Mould the biscuit around the foil to create a vase shape. Carefully remove and shape the second biscuit in the same way. (If this has hardened before you've had time to shape it, return to the oven for a few moments). Make six more vases in the same way.

4. Break up the milk chocolate and melt in a heatproof bowl set over a pan of simmering water. Using a pastry brush, spread the chocolate over the insides of the cases, leaving the edges uncoated.

5. For the coconut custard, put the egg yolks, sugar, cornflour, milk and vanilla essence in a small bowl. Bring the cream and coconut milk to the boil in a saucepan. Immediately pour onto the yolk mixture, stirring. Return to the heat and cook, stirring, for 2 minutes until thickened. Transfer to a bowl and stir in the lemon juice. Cover the surface closely with greaseproof paper to prevent a skin forming and allow to cool.

6. Just before serving, spoon the custard into the lace vases. Dust with cocoa powder and decorate with chocolate curls and coconut shavings.

NOTE: For the coconut shavings, pare curls from a fresh coconut and toast them lightly. Alternatively you could toast bought shredded coconut.

TECHNIQUE

To shape each biscuit, lift over the foil-covered cup and mould around the side with your hands, fluting the edge.

WHITE CHOCOLATE AND BANANA MUSCOVADO CREAMS

A softly peaking blend of cream and yogurt is layered in perfect partnership with a white chocolate and banana purée. Each layer is scattered with dark muscovado sugar which dissolves deliciously into the layers, giving a warm treacly taste. Assemble at least an hour in advance to allow the sugar time to turn syrupy.

SERVES 4

175 g (6 oz) white chocolate
150 ml (¼ pint) double
   cream
2 ripe bananas
20 ml (4 tsp) lemon juice
250 g (9 oz) Greek-style
   yogurt
40 g (1½ oz) dark
   muscovado sugar
TO DECORATE
chocolate caraque or curls,
   (see page 8)

PREPARATION TIME
15 minutes, plus chilling
COOKING TIME
Nil
FREEZING
Not suitable

585 CALS PER SERVING

1. Break up the chocolate and put into a heatproof bowl set over a pan of simmering water. Add 45 ml (3 tbsp) of the cream and leave until melted.

2. Mash the bananas in a bowl, using a fork, then mix in the lemon juice. Transfer to a food processor or blender, add the melted chocolate mixture and process briefly until smooth. (Alternatively thoroughly mash the bananas, add the lemon juice, then beat in the chocolate by hand.) Chill for about 1 hour until firmer in texture.

3. Lightly whip the remaining cream in a bowl, then fold in the yogurt. Spoon a third of the cream mixture into the bases of 4 stemmed serving glasses. Sprinkle with a little of the sugar.

4. Spoon half the banana mixture over the cream and sprinkle with a little more of the sugar. Add another cream layer, then the remaining banana mixture and finally the remaining cream, sprinkling each layer with the sugar. Keep in a cool place until required.

5. Scatter a few chocolate curls on top of each dessert before serving.

NOTE: Use small slender glasses for serving to emphasise the pretty layering.

VARIATION

Mix 5 ml (1 tsp) finely ground espresso coffee with the muscovado sugar before sprinkling.

TECHNIQUE

Briefly process the mashed bananas with the melted chocolate mixture until smooth.

CHOCOLATE CUPS WITH COFFEE SYLLABUB

Circles of melted milk chocolate, loosely draped and set over moulds, make pretty containers for chocolate mousses, custards and other creamy desserts. Here the filling is a whipped syllabub flavoured with espresso coffee and liqueur. Piped chocolate decorations add a professional finishing touch.

SERVES 6

CASES
150 g (5 oz) milk chocolate
15 g (½ oz) unsalted butter
SYLLABUB
90 ml (3 fl oz) strong black coffee
60 ml (4 tbsp) Tia Maria
300 ml (½ pint) double cream
15 ml (1 tbsp) icing sugar
grated rind of 1 lemon
TO FINISH
piped chocolate decorations (see page 10)
cocoa powder, for dusting (optional)

PREPARATION TIME
25 minutes, plus setting and piped decorations
COOKING TIME
Nil
FREEZING
Not suitable

430 CALS PER SERVING

1. For the cases, break up the chocolate and place in a heatproof bowl set over a pan of simmering water. Add the butter and leave until melted. Draw six 12 cm (5 inch) circles on greaseproof paper. Cut out each one, 1 cm (½ inch) outside the drawn circles.

2. Place 6 narrow tumblers, upturned, on a large baking sheet. Spoon half the melted chocolate mixture onto three of the greaseproof paper circles. Using the back of a teaspoon, swirl the chocolate over the circles, making attractive fluted edges which just meet the 12 cm (5 inch) markings.

3. Lift each chocolate-covered circle over a tumbler so that it falls softly around the side. Repeat with the remaining three circles. Chill for at least 1 hour until set firm, then carefully peel away the greaseproof paper. Chill the cases while making the filling.

4. For the syllabub, mix together the coffee and liqueur. Put the cream, icing sugar and lemon rind in a bowl and beat using an electric whisk, until peaking. Gradually blend in the coffee mixture until softly peaking.

5. Spoon the syllabub into the prepared cases, peaking each serving in the centre.

Decorate with piped chocolate decorations and serve at once, dusted with cocoa powder if preferred.

NOTE: Avoid over-whisking the syllabub otherwise it will gradually lose its smooth texture and eventually curdle.

VARIATIONS

Scatter soft fruits or broken walnuts around the syllabub to serve.

TECHNIQUE

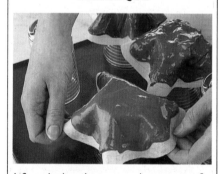

Lift each chocolate-covered greaseproof paper circle over a tumbler so that it flutes softly around the side.

WHITE CHOCOLATE CREAMS WITH RASPBERRIES

In contrast to the rich, dark, voluptuous aura of most chocolate recipes, these prettily presented chocolate pots are rather more mildly flavoured. White chocolate and cream, lightened with the tang of ricotta cheese, is perfectly complemented by the surrounding fruit sauce. Tiny flowerpots make ideal perforated moulds; you can, of course, use heart-shaped *coeur à la crème* dishes instead if you have some.

SERVES 6

CHOCOLATE CREAMS
75 g (3 oz) white chocolate
250 g (9 oz) ricotta cheese
generous pinch of freshly
**   grated nutmeg**
300 ml (½ pint) double
**   cream**
2 egg whites
10 ml (2 tsp) caster sugar
SAUCE
225 g (8 oz) raspberries
30 ml (2 tbsp) kirsch
15-30 ml (1-2 tbsp) icing
**   sugar**
TO SERVE
extra raspberries
chocolate shavings (see
**   page 8)**
freshly grated nutmeg, for
**   sprinkling**

PREPARATION TIME
20 minutes, plus standing
COOKING TIME
Nil
FREEZING
Not suitable

395 CALS PER SERVING

1. Line six perfectly clean small flower-pots, measuring 6 cm (2½ inch) across the top, with pieces of muslin. Finely grate the chocolate.

2. In a bowl, lightly beat the ricotta cheese with the nutmeg until evenly mixed. Add the cream and grated chocolate and beat until the mixture is just peaking.

3. In a separate bowl, whisk the egg whites until stiff, then whisk in the sugar. Using a large metal spoon, fold a quarter of the egg whites into the creamed mixture to loosen it, then carefully fold in the remaining egg whites.

4. Divide the mixture between the prepared pots, packing it down well into the corners. Stand the pots on a tray and chill in the refrigerator for several hours or overnight.

5. For the sauce, put the raspberries, kirsch and 15 ml (1 tbsp) of the icing sugar in a blender or food processor and work until smooth. Pass through a sieve to remove the pips. Taste and add a little more icing sugar if necessary.

6. To serve, invert the chocolate creams onto individual serving plates and peel off the muslin. Spoon the raspberry sauce to one side and scatter with raspberries. Decorate with chocolate shavings and dust lightly with nutmeg.

NOTE: Small terracotta flowerpots, available from garden centres, make perfect individual dessert moulds. Keep a set purely for culinary use.

TECHNIQUE

Using the back of a spoon, pack the chocolate mixture firmly into the muslin-lined flowerpots.

CHOCOLATE ZABAGLIONE

This wonderfully easy dessert, combining whisked egg yolks and Marsala with cocoa powder for a rich glossy texture, is based on a classic Italian Zabaglione. Lightly crushed amaretti biscuits are folded in moments before serving. Their crunchy texture perfectly contrasts the smoothness of the foamy chocolate sauce.

SERVES 6

100 g (3½ oz) amaretti
  biscuits
30 ml (2 tbsp) Marsala
ZABAGLIONE
25 g (1 oz) cocoa powder
5 egg yolks
50 g (2 oz) caster sugar
150 ml (¼ pint) Marsala
TOPPING
50 g (2 oz) plain chocolate
cocoa powder, for dusting
  (optional)

PREPARATION TIME
10 minutes
COOKING TIME
10 minutes
FREEZING
Not suitable

260 CALS PER SERVING

1. Divide half the amaretti biscuits between 6 tall stemmed glasses. Moisten each portion with 5 ml (1 tsp) of Marsala. Crush the remaining biscuits into small pieces and set aside.

2. For the topping, break up the chocolate and melt in a heatproof bowl set over a pan of simmering water.

3. For the zabaglione, put the cocoa, egg yolks and sugar in a large bowl and position over a pan of simmering water. Using an electric whisk, beat until smooth, then gradually whisk in the Marsala. Continue whisking for a further 10 minutes or until the mixture has substantially increased in volume and is slightly foamy.

4. Remove the bowl from the pan. Fold the crushed biscuits into the whisked mixture and spoon into the serving glasses. Spoon a little of the melted chocolate over each dessert and swirl lightly with a cocktail stick. Serve immediately, dusted with cocoa powder if desired. Or leave to cool before serving.

NOTE: The mixture may take a while to start increasing in volume as you whisk it, but it should be sufficiently aerated after about 10 minutes.

VARIATION

Use a medium sweet sherry in place of the Marsala. Crushed macaroons can be used instead of the amaretti biscuits.

TECHNIQUE

Continue whisking the mixture until it is slightly paler in colour, increased in volume and quite foamy.

RICH CHOCOLATE MOUSSE CUPS

Only chocolate, with its unique texture, could be set into such stunning shapes as these dessert cases. Smoothly rounded yet attractively jagged at the edges, they are most impressive. The rich, velvety smooth, chocolate mousse filling is flavoured with rum or brandy. Serve with a casual decoration of seasonal fruits.

SERVES 6

CASES
225 g (8 oz) plain chocolate
MOUSSE
200 g (7 oz) plain chocolate
I egg, separated
25 g (1 oz) unsalted butter
30 ml (2 tbsp) rum or
  brandy
150 ml (¼ pint) double
  cream
15 ml (1 tbsp) caster sugar
TO SERVE
selection of fruits
mint sprigs to decorate
icing sugar, for dusting

PREPARATION TIME
35 minutes, plus setting
COOKING TIME
Nil
FREEZING
Suitable

560 CALS PER SERVING

1. Break up the chocolate and melt in a heatproof bowl set over a pan of simmering water. Line a baking sheet with greaseproof paper. Cut six 30 × 12 cm (12 × 5 inch) strips of greaseproof paper; fold each in half lengthways.

2. Roll a greaseproof paper strip into a circle and shape inside a 6 cm (2½ inch) pastry cutter set on a baking sheet, with the folded edge on the base. Secure the ends with tape. Remove the cutter and shape 5 more collars in the same way.

3. Place the cutter on one collar. Spoon a little melted chocolate into the base and brush most of the way up the sides to make a case with jagged edges. Carefully remove the cutter and repeat with the remaining collars. Leave the chocolate cases in a cool place to set firmly.

4. To prepare the mousse, break up the chocolate and place in a heatproof bowl set over a pan of simmering water. Add the egg yolk and butter and leave until melted. Remove from the heat and stir in the rum or brandy.

5. Lightly whip the cream. In another bowl, whisk the egg white until stiff, then gradually whisk in the sugar. Fold the cream into the chocolate mixture, then fold in the whisked egg white.

6. Divide the mousse mixture between the chocolate cases and chill until firm.

7. To serve, carefully peel away the paper. Place the cases on individual serving plates with a small arrangement of fruits alongside. Decorate with mint sprigs and dust lightly with icing sugar.

NOTE: Avoid making the cases too thick, particularly over the bases. Any leftover chocolate from the cases can be added to the mousse.

VARIATION

Omit the rum or brandy. Add 30 ml (2 tbsp) freshly chopped mint to the mousse instead.

TECHNIQUE

Use a pastry brush to spread the choco-late up the side of each collar, to create an attractive jagged edge.

CHOCOLATE MARQUISE WITH CARAMEL KUMQUATS

This recipe epitomises a chocolate dessert at its richest, creamiest, smoothest and most tempting. Lightened with whipped cream and laced with orange liqueur, plain and white chocolate are marbled together and chilled until firm enough to slice. Both the Marquise and accompanying kumquats are best prepared a day ahead.

SERVES 6-8

MARQUISE
200 g (7 oz) plain chocolate
125 g (4 oz) white chocolate
45 ml (3 tbsp) Cointreau or other orange liqueur
75 g (3 oz) unsalted butter, softened
50 g (2 oz) icing sugar
15 ml (1 tbsp) cocoa powder
300 ml (½ pint) double cream

CARAMEL KUMQUATS
350 g (12 oz) kumquats
175 g (6 oz) caster sugar

TO DECORATE
mint sprigs

PREPARATION TIME
30 minutes, plus chilling
COOKING TIME
10-15 minutes
FREEZING
Suitable: Marquise only

795-600 CALS PER SERVING

1. Line a 450 g (1 lb) loaf tin with cling film. Break up the plain and white chocolate; keep separate. Put the plain chocolate into a heatproof bowl set over a pan of simmering water. Add 30 ml (2 tbsp) of the liqueur and leave until melted. Melt the white chocolate with the remaining 15 ml (1 tbsp) liqueur in the same way.

2. Beat 50 g (2 oz) of the butter and 25 g (1 oz) of the icing sugar together in a bowl until pale and creamy. Sift in the cocoa, add the melted plain chocolate and fold in until evenly incorporated. In a separate bowl, lightly whip the cream; fold half into the plain chocolate mixture.

3. Beat the remaining butter and icing sugar together in another bowl. Stir in the white chocolate, then fold in the remaining cream.

4. Place alternate spoonfuls of the two mixtures in the prepared tin. Tap tin gently to level surface. Chill the Marquise for several hours or overnight.

5. For the caramel kumquats, prick the kumquats all over with a fork and place in a saucepan with 600 ml (1 pint) water. Bring to the boil, reduce the heat and simmer gently for 5 minutes until softened. Drain the kumquats, reserving the liquid.

6. Return 350 ml (12 fl oz) of the liquid to a heavy-based saucepan. Add the sugar and heat gently until dissolved. Bring to the boil and boil rapidly until the syrup turns a deep caramel. Plunge the base of the pan into cold water to stop further cooking. Carefully add 75 ml (3 fl oz) boiling water to the caramel and heat gently until dissolved. Pour over the kumquats and chill until ready to serve.

7. Thinly slice the Marquise and arrange on individual serving plates with the kumquats in caramel. Decorate with mint and serve at once.

VARIATIONS

Replace caramel kumquats with fresh, strawberries, raspberries or peaches.

TECHNIQUE

Using a spoon, layer the two chocolate mixtures in the tin, alternating the colours.

CHOCOLATE CINNAMON MOUSSE CAKE

The appealing, sugar-crusted, cracked exterior of this cake rather belies the soft, soufflé-textured consistency within. This is achieved using a whisked egg mixture, rich with chocolate and lightly spiced with cinnamon. During cooking it rises dramatically, then deflates while cooling to acquire its wonderful mousse-like texture.

SERVES 8

225 g (8 oz) plain chocolate
125 g (4 oz) unsalted butter
30 ml (2 tbsp) brandy
5 eggs, separated
125 g (4 oz) caster sugar
5 ml (1 tsp) ground
cinnamon
TO DECORATE
50 g (2 oz) plain chocolate
125 g (4 oz) strawberries
two-tone chocolate caraque
(see page 8)
icing sugar, for dusting

PREPARATION TIME
25 minutes, plus cooling and
chocolate caraque
COOKING TIME
30-40 minutes
FREEZING
Not suitable

455 CALS PER SERVING

1. Preheat the oven to 160°C (325°F) Mark 3. Grease and line a 23 cm (9 inch) spring-release cake tin.

2. Break up the chocolate and place in a heatproof bowl over a pan of simmering water. Add the butter and leave until melted. Remove from the heat, add the brandy and stir until smooth.

3. Place the egg yolks in a bowl with 75 g (3 oz) of the sugar. Whisk until the mixture is pale and thick enough to leave a thin trail on the surface when the whisk is lifted from the bowl. Stir in the melted chocolate mixture.

4. In a separate bowl, whisk the egg whites until stiff. Gradually whisk in the remaining sugar, adding the cinnamon with the final addition of sugar. Using a large metal spoon, fold a quarter of the egg whites into the chocolate mixture to loosen it, then carefully fold in the remainder.

5. Turn the mixture into the prepared tin. Bake for 30-40 minutes until well risen and the centre feels just spongy when gently pressed. Leave to cool in the tin.

6. Transfer the cake to a serving plate, peeling away the lining paper. For the decoration, break up the chocolate and melt in a heatproof bowl set over a pan of simmering water. Dip the strawberries in the chocolate to half-coat (see page 11). Casually pile the chocolate curls and strawberries onto the cake and dust lightly with icing sugar to serve.

NOTE: The undecorated cake will keep well in the refrigerator for 2-3 days. Leave at room temperature for 30 minutes before serving.

TECHNIQUE

Carefully fold the remaining egg whites into the chocolate mixture until only just incorporated.

ICED CHOCOLATE INDULGENCE

Resembling a 'Mille Feuille' with its layers and lavish filling, this stunning, prepare-ahead dessert is ideal for a party gathering. Wafer-thin rectangles of bitter chocolate sandwich an airy ice-cream, partially flavoured with chocolate shavings, espresso coffee, toasted hazelnuts and coffee liqueur.

SERVES 8

ICE CREAM
25 g (1 oz) plain chocolate
75 g (3 oz) unblanched hazelnuts
15-30 ml (1-2 tbsp) finely ground espresso coffee, to taste
6 eggs, separated
175 g (6 oz) caster sugar
300 ml (½ pint) double cream

TO FINISH
150 g (5 oz) bitter chocolate
15 ml (1 tbsp) double cream
25 g (1 oz) white chocolate
milk chocolate curls (see page 8)

PREPARATION TIME
45 minutes, plus freezing and chocolate curls
COOKING TIME
Nil
FREEZING
Suitable

540 CALS PER SERVING

1. Set the freezer to fast-freeze. Preheat the grill. For the ice-cream, roughly grate the chocolate. Roughly chop the hazelnuts and toast until evenly golden. Mix the ground coffee with 30 ml (2 tbsp) boiling water.

2. Whisk the egg yolks and 75 g (3 oz) of the sugar in a bowl until pale and fluffy.

3. Whip the cream until just holding its shape. In a separate bowl, whisk the egg whites until stiff, then gradually whisk in the remaining sugar. Using a large metal spoon, fold the cream into the yolk mixture, then fold in the whisked egg whites. Turn half the mixture into a freezer-proof container.

4. Fold the grated chocolate, 50 g (2 oz) of the hazelnuts and the coffee into the remaining mixture. Turn into a separate freezerproof container. Freeze both mixtures for 2-3 hours or until firm.

5. For the chocolate layers, break up the bitter chocolate and put into a heat-proof bowl over a pan of simmering water. Add the cream; leave until melted. Melt the white chocolate separately.

6. Draw 4 rectangles, each measuring 18×9 cm (7×3½ inches), on grease-proof paper. Spread the bitter chocolate evenly over the rectangles giving each attractive fluted edges which just extend over the markings. Using a teaspoon, flick the white chocolate over one rectangle and feather lightly. Leave to set.

7. To assemble the dessert, you will need to work quite quickly. Layer up the chocolate rectangles and ice-cream on a serving plate, alternating soft scoops of plain and coffee ice-cream, and sprinkling each layer with hazelnuts and chocolate curls. Finish with the feathered chocolate rectangle.

8. Scatter any remaining hazelnuts and chocolate curls around the dessert. Cover loosely and return to the freezer. Transfer to the refrigerator 10 minutes before serving to soften slightly.

TECHNIQUE

Flick the white chocolate over one rectangle. Immediately feather it into the dark chocolate, using a cocktail stick.

CHOCOLATE BOWL WITH DIPPED FRUITS AND NUTS

This beautifully sculptured bowl takes full advantage of the way in which chocolate can be melted, moulded and set into virtually any shape. The more ruffled, rugged and textured the bowl the more impressive it looks when filled with fruits, nuts or confectionery. For convenience, make the bowl a few days in advance.

SERVES 8

CHOCOLATE BOWL
225 g (8 oz) plain chocolate
DIPPED FRUIT AND NUTS
150 g (5 oz) plain chocolate
450 g (1 lb) strawberries
125 g (4 oz) red cherries
125 g (4 oz) cape
   gooseberries
50 g (2 oz) brazil nuts

PREPARATION TIME
30 minutes, plus setting
COOKING TIME
Nil
FREEZING
Not suitable

340 CALS PER SERVING

1. Melt the chocolate in a heatproof bowl set over a pan of simmering water. Cut two 30 cm (12 inch) squares from heavy-duty kitchen foil. Place one on top of the other and fold the edges together to secure. Place over an upturned 750 ml (1¼ pint) mixing bowl and mould the foil around the bowl, smoothing out the creases and letting the ends curve away from the bowl.

2. Carefully release the foil from the bowl, retaining the shape. Turn the foil bowl the right way up and press down lightly on the surface to create a flat base.

3. Using a teaspoon, spread the chocolate over the inside of the foil, easing it up the sides in an even layer, and making an attractive ragged edge around the top. Chill in the refrigerator for at least 30 minutes.

4. Melt the chocolate for dipping (as above). Use to half coat the fruits and nuts (see page 11). Chill in the refrigerator or leave in a cool place until set.

5. Carefully peel the foil away from the chocolate bowl, starting at the top and working down to the base. (If it starts to soften with the heat of your hands, return to the refrigerator to firm up.)

6. Pile the dipped fruits and nuts into the chocolate bowl and keep in a cool place until ready to serve.

NOTE: If the melted chocolate for the bowl is too warm it will run down the sides of the foil into the base. If so, leave for 5-10 minutes and try again.

VARIATIONS

Use the chocolate bowl as a serving dish for any of the confectionery in this chapter, particularly the Truffles, Irish Coffee Cups and Chocolate Marzipan Pecans. Alternatively, use the bowl to hold a firm-textured mousse. Individual bowls also work well; use oranges or individual pudding basins as moulds.

TECHNIQUE

Spread the melted chocolate over the base and up the sides of the foil bowl until coated in a fairly thick, even layer.

IRISH COFFEE CUPS

Miniature petit four cases make perfect moulds for shaping small chocolates. These delicate chocolate cups cleverly conceal two complimentary layers: one smooth, white and creamy; the other fudge-like and flavoured with coffee and brandy. Enjoyable to assemble, though slightly fiddly, they can be made several days in advance and stored in a cool place until required.

MAKES 22

CASES
175 g (6 oz) plain chocolate
FILLING
75 g (3 oz) white chocolate
50 ml (2 fl oz) double cream
75 g (3 oz) plain chocolate
10 ml (2 tsp) finely ground
   espresso coffee
15 ml (1 tbsp) brandy
TO DECORATE
40 g (1½ oz) white
   chocolate

PREPARATION TIME
40 minutes, plus setting
COOKING TIME
Nil
FREEZING
Not suitable

100 CALS PER CUP

1. For the cases, break up 125 g (4 oz) of the plain chocolate and melt in a heat-proof bowl set over a pan of simmering water. Separate 20 small foil or paper petit four cases. (Use double thickness paper cases to make coating easier).

2. Spoon a little chocolate into a case and spread evenly over the base and around the sides, using the back of a tea-spoon. Invert onto a greaseproof paper lined tray. Coat the remaining cases in the same way and leave in a cool place to set. Turn the set cases the right way up.

3. For the filling, break up the white chocolate and place in a small saucepan with the cream. Heat gently until the chocolate is melted. Remove from the heat and beat lightly. Use the cream mixture to half-fill the chocolate cases.

4. Break up the plain chocolate and melt in a separate bowl. Mix the coffee with 15 ml (1 tbsp) hot water. Add to the melted chocolate with the brandy and stir until smooth. Spoon over the white chocolate until only the rim of the chocolate case remains visible above the level of the filling.

5. Melt the remaining 50 g (2 oz) plain chocolate for the cases as above. Melt the white chocolate for decoration, place in a greaseproof piping bag and snip off the tip.

6. Spread a little plain chocolate on the surface of one of the cups. Pipe a little white chocolate on top and immediately feather, using a cocktail stick. Repeat on the remaining cups. Keep in a cool place until ready to serve.

NOTE: Make sure the filling mixtures are not too warm when you fill the cases, otherwise they may melt the cases.

The quantity made will vary according to the size of the petit four cases used. Those measuring 3 cm (1¼ inches) in diameter across the top are ideal. Any leftover white chocolate filling can be lightly whipped and spooned onto the set cups. Flick with a knife to peak attractively, then dust lightly with cocoa.

TECHNIQUE

Spoon a little melted chocolate into the cases and spread with the back of a small teaspoon until evenly covered. Invert onto a greaseproof paper lined tray and leave to set.

FRESH CREAM TRUFFLES

These sensational creamy truffles are the ultimate taste in chocolate. Few can resist the characteristic velvet smooth blend of melt-in-the-mouth chocolate and rich cream, flavoured with brandy or liqueur. Casually pile cocoa or sugar dusted truffles onto a serving dish or try variations on textures and flavours for an eye-catching after-dinner assortment.

MAKES 20

175 g (6 oz) plain chocolate
120 ml (4 fl oz) double
**   cream**
30 ml (2 tbsp) brandy,
**   Cointreau or other**
**   orange liqueur**
cocoa powder or icing
**   sugar, for dusting**

PREPARATION TIME
15 minutes, plus chilling
COOKING TIME
Nil
FREEZING
Not suitable

85 CALS PER TRUFFLE

1. Break the chocolate into small pieces. Put the cream in a small saucepan and bring slowly to the boil. Remove from the heat and stir in the chocolate until melted and smooth. Stir in the brandy or liqueur.

2. Transfer the mixture to a bowl and leave to cool for about 30 minutes. At this stage, whisk the mixture until it is slightly paler and holds its shape. Chill in the refrigerator until firm enough to handle.

3. Dust your hands with cocoa powder or icing sugar and shape the truffle mixture into small balls, about 2 cm (¾ inch) in diameter. Roll in cocoa powder or icing sugar to coat. Chill in the refrigerator until required.

NOTE: Make sure hands, work surface and any utensils used for shaping truffles are cool and thoroughly dusted in icing sugar or cocoa.

These truffles may be stored in the refrigerator for up to 3 days. Dust with a little extra icing sugar or cocoa powder if necessary.

VARIATIONS

● Use bitter, white or milk, instead of plain chocolate.
● Replace the brandy or orange liqueur with other flavours, such as Tia Maria blended with 5 ml (1 tsp) finely ground espresso coffee.
● For non-alcoholic truffles, omit the brandy or liqueur and stir in 30 ml (2 tbsp) finely chopped nuts or crushed praline before shaping the mixture.
● For chocolate dipped truffles, chill the truffle balls, then dip in melted white, milk or plain chocolate. Roll across a fine grid cooling rack to ruffle the surface. Alternatively texture the surface with a fork.

TECHNIQUE

Beat the cooled truffle mixture, using an electric whisk, until it is slightly paler and holds its shape.

CHOCOLATE MARZIPAN PECANS

Laced with brandy and the bitter-sweet flavour of cocoa, these pecan-flavoured marzipan sweets are easy to make, yet smart enough to hand round after a dinner party. Whole pecans and smooth milk chocolate add the finishing touch, although plain or bitter chocolate could be substituted for a less sweet variation.

MAKES 20

125 g (4 oz) shelled pecan
   nuts
40 g (1½ oz) caster sugar
40 g (1½ oz) icing sugar
15 ml (1 tbsp) cocoa powder
10 ml (2 tsp) brandy
1 egg white
TO DECORATE
75 g (3 oz) milk chocolate
20 shelled pecan nuts, about
   40 g (1½ oz)

PREPARATION TIME
20 minutes, plus standing
COOKING TIME
Nil
FREEZING
Not suitable

95 CALS PER SWEET

1. Put the pecans in a food processor or blender and work to the consistency of ground almonds. Transfer to a bowl and add the caster sugar, icing sugar and cocoa powder. Stir until evenly combined, then mix in the brandy.

2. Beat the egg white lightly with a fork, and add 15 ml (1 tbsp) to the pecan mixture. Mix to a paste, adding a little more egg white if the mixture is too dry.

3. Lightly knead the paste and shape into a cylindrical log, about 3 cm (1¼ inches) thick. Slice the log widthways into 20 even-sized pieces.

4. Break up the chocolate and melt in a heatproof bowl set over a pan of simmering water. Using a teaspoon, spoon a little melted chocolate onto each sweet and top with a pecan half.

5. Transfer the sweets to a serving plate and leave in a cool place for 1-2 hours before serving.

NOTE: Avoid over-kneading the paste before shaping, otherwise it will develop an oily texture.

VARIATIONS

Use walnuts or brazil nuts instead of the pecans. Replace the brandy with orange or coffee-flavoured liqueur.

TECHNIQUE

Using a sharp knife, cut the log into 20 even-sized pieces.

WHITE CHOCOLATE COATED BRANDIED FRUITS

Finely chopped dried fruits, generously steeped in brandy, are enveloped in toasted coconut and creamy white chocolate. These simple sweets, in contrast to bitter-sweet dark chocolate confectionery, should earn wide appeal with the sweet-toothed. For best results use the most luxurious white chocolate available.

MAKES 30

50 g (2 oz) dried pears
25 g (1 oz) dried apples
50 g (2 oz) dried peaches
60 ml (4 tbsp) brandy
25 g (1 oz) desiccated
   coconut
125 g (4 oz) white chocolate
TO DECORATE
40 g (1½ oz) white
   chocolate

PREPARATION TIME
20 minutes, plus standing
COOKING TIME
Nil
FREEZING
Not suitable

45 CALS PER SWEET

1. Chop the pears, apples and peaches as finely as possible, preferably in a food processor. Transfer to a bowl and stir in the brandy. Pack the mixture down lightly and leave to stand for 30 minutes to 1 hour until the brandy has been absorbed.

2. Preheat the grill and toast the coconut until evenly golden. Break up the chocolate and melt in a heatproof bowl set over a pan of simmering water. Add the melted chocolate to the fruits with the coconut and stir until the ingredients are evenly combined.

3. Take heaped teaspoonfuls of the mixture and shape into ovals, about 3 cm (1¼ inches) long. Place on a baking sheet or tray lined with greaseproof paper.

4. To decorate the sweets, melt the chocolate as above and place in a greaseproof paper piping bag. Snip off the tip and pipe diagonal lines over the top and sides of the chocolates. Leave to set, then place in paper sweet cases.

NOTE: If the mixture sets in the bowl before you've had time to shape the sweets, heat it in the microwave for a few moments.

VARIATIONS

Replace half the coconut with skinned and finely chopped pistachio nuts. Use dark chocolate to decorate the sweets.

TECHNIQUE

Shape the fruit mixture into small ovals and place slightly apart on a greaseproof paper lined baking sheet or tray.

CHOCOLATE FUDGE STICKS

Plain chocolate gives fudge a superior flavour and a smoother, creamier texture than the more frequently used cocoa powder. Once decorated, allow these fudge sticks time to stand, uncovered, so that they can develop a slight crust. Rich, yet slender and so more-ish to eat, they'll disappear fast!

MAKES 60

100 g (3½ oz) plain
   chocolate
225 g (8 oz) granulated
   sugar
395 g (14 oz) can sweetened
   condensed milk
50 g (2 oz) unsalted butter
15 ml (1 tbsp) clear honey
5 ml (1 tsp) vanilla essence
TO DECORATE
40 g (1½ oz) milk or plain
   chocolate

PREPARATION TIME
15 minutes, plus cooling
COOKING TIME
6-8 minutes
FREEZING
Not suitable

55 CALS PER SWEET

1. Grease a 20 cm (8 inch) loose-bottomed square cake tin and line the base and 2.5 cm (1 inch) up the sides with non-stick baking parchment. Finely grate the chocolate.

2. Put the sugar, condensed milk, butter, honey and vanilla essence in a medium, heavy-based saucepan and heat gently until the sugar dissolves. Bring to the boil, stirring frequently, and boil for 6-8 minutes or until the mixture reaches the 'soft ball stage' (see technique), and the temperature registers 115°C (240°F) on a sugar thermometer.

3. Remove the pan from the heat, add the grated chocolate and beat until the mixture is smooth and glossy. Pour the fudge into the prepared tin, spreading it into the corners. Leave for 2 hours or until completely set.

4. Remove the fudge from the tin and peel away the paper lining the sides. Cut the fudge into 60 fingers. Separate the fudge sticks and arrange on a baking sheet or tray lined with greaseproof paper.

5. To decorate the fudge, break up the chocolate and melt in a heatproof bowl set over a pan of simmering water. Transfer to a greaseproof paper piping bag, snip off the end and pipe lines haphazardly over the fudge. Leave to set.

NOTE: Because of the high sugar content, the fudge is prone to sticking to the pan during boiling. Stir frequently and lower the temperature if necessary to prevent this happening.

VARIATIONS

Add 50 g (2 oz) of chopped walnuts, or 25 g (1 oz) chopped raisins and 15 ml (1 tbsp) rum to the fudge, after stirring in the chocolate.

TECHNIQUE

To test for the 'soft ball stage', drop a teaspoonful of the mixture into a bowl of cold water. It should then be possible to roll it between the fingers into a soft ball.

BITTER SWEET CHOCOLATE NUT SLICE

An indulgent speciality for chocolate connoisseurs. Lightly specked with toasted almonds, stem ginger and raisins, and subtly flavoured with brandy, bitter chocolate can be relished in virtually unadulterated bliss! Once made, the roll can be refrigerated for up to a week, ready for thinly slicing off pieces as required.

MAKES 30 SLICES

40 g (1½ oz) blanched
  almonds
15 g (½ oz) stem ginger
25 g (1 oz) raisins,
  preferably lexia
100 g (3½ oz) bitter
  chocolate
40 g (1½ oz) unsalted butter
30 ml (2 tbsp) brandy
TO DECORATE
75 g (3 oz) flaked almonds
75 g (3 oz) white chocolate

PREPARATION TIME
20 minutes, plus setting
COOKING TIME
Nil
FREEZING
Not suitable

60 CALS PER SLICE

1. Preheat the grill. Finely chop the almonds and lightly toast them. Finely dice the stem ginger. Roughly chop the raisins. Break up the chocolate and put into a heatproof bowl set over a pan of simmering water. Add the butter and leave until melted.

2. Add the toasted almonds, ginger, raisins and brandy to the melted chocolate and stir gently until evenly mixed.

3. Lay a sheet of greaseproof paper on the work surface and spoon the chocolate mixture across the centre. Wrap the greaseproof paper around the chocolate, shaping it into a roll, about 3 cm (1¼ inches) wide. Fold under the ends of the paper. Chill the roll in the refrigerator for 2 hours or until firm.

4. For the decoration, crush the almonds until broken into slightly smaller pieces, then lightly toast them. Break up the white chocolate and melt in a heatproof bowl set over a pan of simmering water.

5. Unwrap the chocolate roll. Using a palette knife quickly spread the white chocolate all over the surface of the log, then roll in the almonds until evenly covered. Chill for a further 1 hour until set. Serve cut into thin slices.

VARIATIONS

For a sweeter alternative, use milk or white rather than plain chocolate. Substitute chopped candied peel for the stem ginger.

TECHNIQUE

Coat the log with the melted white chocolate, then immediately roll in the toasted almonds to cover evenly. It is essential to work quickly as the white chocolate will soon set firmly.

TOASTED ALMOND AND CHOCOLATE BRITTLE CAKE

A layer of creamy white chocolate, speckled with milk chocolate chips and toasted almonds, is hidden within a richly contrasting coat of bitter chocolate. Rather like a panforte, this delicious confection is set in a shallow rice paper case, making a sophisticated after-dinner treat. Before serving, use the point of a sturdy knife to break the cake into brittle chunks and expose its rugged texture.

MAKES ABOUT 24 PIECES

100 g (3½ oz) blanched
   almonds
50 g (2 oz) milk chocolate
200 g (7 oz) bitter chocolate
200 g (7 oz) white chocolate
1 small orange
30 ml (2 tbsp) Cointreau or
   other orange liqueur

PREPARATION TIME
25 minutes, plus setting
COOKING TIME
Nil
FREEZING
Not suitable

125 CALS PER PIECE

1. Line the base and 1 cm (½ inch) up the side of an 18 cm (7 inch) round cake tin with rice paper (using the same technique as you would for lining a tin with grease-proof paper).

2. Preheat the grill and toast the almonds, turning occasionally, until evenly golden, then chop into large chunks. Roughly chop the milk chocolate.

3. Break up the bitter chocolate and melt in a heatproof bowl set over a pan of simmering water. Spread half the melted chocolate over the base and lined side of the prepared tin.

4. Melt the white chocolate in a separate bowl (as above) and allow to cool. Finely pare the rind from the orange into thin strips, using a citrus zester. Lightly stir the orange rind into the melted white chocolate, together with the liqueur. Stir in half the almonds and half the milk chocolate pieces.

5. Spoon the white chocolate mixture over the bitter chocolate base, almost to the edge of the tin. Cover with the remaining melted bitter chocolate. Immediately sprinkle with the rest of the nuts and milk chocolate, pressing them down into the cake.

6. Leave in a cool place for at least 4 hours until set. Remove from the tin and break into chunks to serve.

NOTE: Make sure the white chocolate is cool before adding the milk chocolate pieces, otherwise the colours will blend together.

VARIATION

Sprinkle the bitter chocolate base with 10 ml (2 tsp) finely ground espresso coffee before applying the white chocolate layer. Use brandy instead of the orange liqueur.

TECHNIQUE

Spoon the white chocolate mixture over the bitter chocolate base, working quickly before the white chocolate begins to set.

Specialist cake decorating equipment, including couverture chocolate and gold lustre powder can be obtained by mail order from SQUIRES KITCHEN, Squires House, 3 Waverley Lane, Farnham, Surrey GL9 8BB Tel 0252 711749/734309.

If you would like further information about the **Good Housekeeping Cookery Club**, please write to: Penny Smith, Ebury Press, Random House, 20 Vauxhall Bridge Road, London SW1V 2SA.